creative
two-block quilts

• 12 ORIGINAL BLOCKS • 20 QUILT DESIGNS • UNLIMITED COMBINATIONS

TRICE BOERENS

C&T PUBLISHING

Text copyright © 2009 by **Trice Boerens**

Artwork copyright © 2009 by **C&T Publishing, Inc.**

Publisher: **Amy Marson**

Creative Director: **Gailen Runge**

Acquisitions Editor: **Susanne Woods**

Editor: **Liz Aneloski**

Technical Editors: **Teresa Stroin** and **Mary E. Flynn**

Copyeditor/Proofreader: **Wordfirm Inc.**

Cover Designer: **Kristen Yenche**

Book Designer: **Rose Sheifer-Wright**

Production Coordinator: **Kirstie L. Pettersen**

Production Editor: **Julia Cianci**

Illustrator: **Trice Boerens**

Photography by **Christina Carty-Francis** and **Diane Pedersen** of C&T Publishing, Inc., unless otherwise noted.

Published by C&T Publishing, Inc., P.O. Box 1456, Lafayette, CA 94549

Library of Congress Cataloging-in-Publication Data

Boerens, Trice.

 Creative two-block quilts : 12 original blocks, 20 quilt designs, unlimited combinations / Trice Boerens.

   p. cm.

 ISBN 978-1-57120-786-9 (soft cover)

 1. Patchwork--Patterns. 2. Quilting--Patterns. I. Title.

 TT835.B6133 2009

 746.46'041--dc22

                              2009011178

Printed in China

10 9 8 7 6 5 4 3 2 1

contents

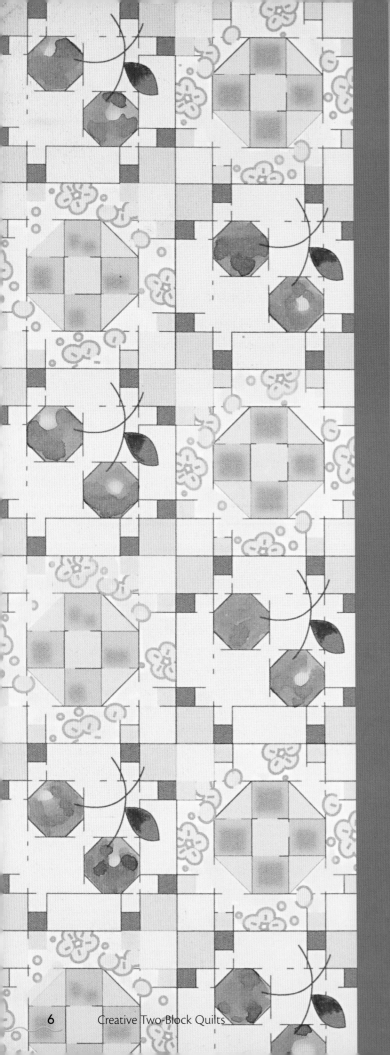

Introduction

Pick two numbers between 1 and 12, and guess what? You win! In fact, you can't lose when you choose from this lively collection of 10" × 10" building blocks. The blocks are dressed-up versions of dressed-down favorites such as the Pin Wheel, the Log Cabin, and the Ohio Star. Play this mix-and-match game and don't stop until you have tried many merry combinations. The fun never ends!

General Instructions

Selecting the Fabrics

Choose 100% cotton fabrics that are soft to the touch and colorfast. As a general rule, use small patterns for small pieces. When a dramatic effect is desired, use complementary colors and combine light and dark values. For a subtle appearance, use colors that are close in hue, value, and pattern scale.

Cutting the Pieces

The measurements specified for the block pieces include a ¼" seam allowance. The template patterns also include a ¼" seam allowance. Be accurate in cutting and sewing the pieces together in order to match the pieced seams.

Yardages are based on 44"-wide fabrics with trimmed selvage edges.

To make paper templates, trace around the printed shapes in the book and cut along the marked lines. Place the templates on the wrong side of the fabric and align the straight sides of the piece with the grain of the fabric. Draw around the shapes with a regular or a colored pencil.

Piecing

To secure fabric layers for piecing, use dressmaker's pins or basting stitches. Pinning is quicker but less accurate. For more accuracy, use plenty of pins and insert them perpendicular to the seamline. Slowly feed the pinned fabric under the presser foot or remove the pins before they reach the presser foot. Basting stitches are large over/under running stitches that are inserted by hand and removed after the machine stitching is complete. Use contrasting thread for easy removal of the basting stitches. Trim the thread ends often while making each block; then trim them again when the block is complete. Also, press the seams often as you work.

Hand Appliqué

Pin the appliqué piece in place. Use a fine sharp needle and short lengths of thread. Turn the edge under at the fold line, then whipstitch the edge to the quilt block. Work in short sections, using small, evenly placed stitches. Crease the fabric with your fingers as you stitch.

Machine Embroidery

If you are using lightweight or loose-weave fabric, pin nonwoven interfacing to the back of the fabric before you begin stitching. If you are using medium-weight cotton fabric, however, reinforcement is not necessary. On a practice scrap of fabric, adjust the machine for the desired stitch width and spacing. Stitch along the marked line. When the stitching is complete, pull the ends of the thread to the wrong side of the fabric and trim. If you used interfacing, trim it close to the stitching line.

Marking the Quilt Top

If you choose to follow the piecing pattern or if you desire a free-form design, it is not necessary to mark the quilt top. If you choose to add a design with the quilting stitches, mark the quilt top before layering it with the batting and the backing. Marks from an air-soluble pen will slowly fade until they disappear entirely. Because the ink fades, use this type of pen only if you plan to complete your quilting that day. Marks from a water-soluble pen will disappear only when misted or blotted with water. Often after misting, the ink from a water-soluble pen will be absorbed by the batting and will then reappear on the quilt top. It may require several treatments to remove this type of ink.

Layering for Quilting

Cut or piece the backing to the same size as the batting. Place the backing on the work surface, wrong side up. Place the quilt batting on the backing and the quilt top on the batting, right side up.

Pinning and Basting for Quilting

To secure the quilt backing, batting, and top before quilting, work from the center out and pin with safety pins or quilter's pins. Or use large hand-basting stitches to hold the layers in place.

Hand Quilting

For hand quilting, attach the layers to the quilting frame or place them in a large hoop. Use a fine, sharp needle and short lengths of quilting thread. Knot the thread end and insert the needle from the back to the front. Quilt with short, even running stitches. At the end of the length, make a small knot and pull the thread to hide the knot under the quilt top inside the batting.

Machine Quilting

Machine quilting requires a sewing table that is large enough to accommodate the quilt's size and weight. Adjust the machine to the desired stitch length. Double stitch the ends of the stitching lines; then work from the center out, using both hands to hold the quilt in place as you feed it through the machine. Stitch at a slower speed than that of normal sewing and roll the quilt as it accumulates under the machine arm. Pull the thread ends to the back of the quilt and trim.

Binding

Choose premade, double-fold bias binding or make your own bias binding by cutting 2⅛"-wide bias strips. Sew the strips together with diagonal seams, angling all the seams in the same direction. Press the seams open.

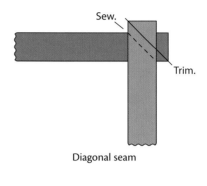

Diagonal seam

Press open.

Trim the batting and backing even with the quilt top. Fold and press the binding in half lengthwise, wrong sides together. Align the raw edges of the binding with the raw edge of the quilt top. Leave the first few inches of the binding unattached and sew the rest of the binding to the quilt. At the corners, stop ¼" from the edge, lift the presser foot, and fold the binding up and down at a right angle. Turn the quilt and the binding, realign the edges, and continue stitching.

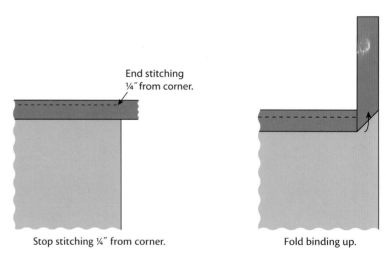

Stop stitching ¼" from corner.

Fold binding up.

Fold binding down.

Sew around the entire outside edge of the quilt. At the point where you started, fold under the raw end of the binding ¼" to the wrong side. Then place the opposite end of the binding inside the folded end and sew in place.

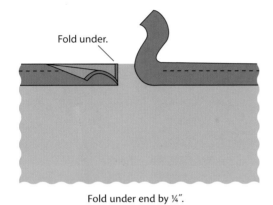

Fold under.

Fold under end by ¼".

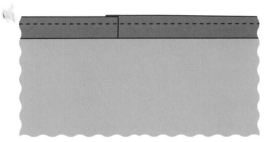

Place opposite end inside folded end and sew.

Fold the binding around the quilt's edges and hand stitch the folded edge of the binding to the back of the quilt. At the corners, fold under the binding at a diagonal to make a mitered corner.

The Blocks
and Quilts

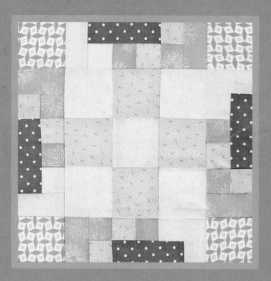

BLOCK 1

FABRIC REQUIREMENTS

Amounts listed are for 18 blocks because featured quilts (pages 26–31) are assembled with 35 blocks—18 of one block and 17 of another.

Light yellow print: ⅞ yard

Light blue print: ¾ yard

Blue polka dot: ⅓ yard

Pink print: ½ yard

Cream/pink print: ½ yard

CUTTING

Light yellow print

Cut 6 strips 2½" × fabric width, then cut into 90 squares 2½" × 2½" (A).

Cut 7 strips 1½" × fabric width, then cut into 72 squares 1½" × 1½" (F) and 72 rectangles 1½" × 2½" (H).

Light blue print

Cut 5 strips 2½" × fabric width, then cut into 72 squares 2½" × 2½" (B).

Cut 5 strips 1½" × fabric width, then cut into 144 squares 1½" × 1½" (D).

Blue polka dot

Cut 6 strips 1½" × fabric width, then cut into 72 rectangles 1½" × 3½" (G).

Pink print

Cut 10 strips 1½" × fabric width, then cut into 144 squares 1½" × 1½" (C) and 72 rectangles 1½" × 2½" (E).

Cream/pink print

Cut 5 strips 2½" × fabric width, then cut into 72 squares 2½" × 2½" (I).

BLOCK CONSTRUCTION

Instructions are for constructing one block.

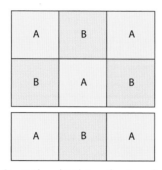

1. Sew 5 A's and 4 B's together to make a nine-patch unit.

2. Sew C to D. Add E. Make 4.

3. Sew D, C, and F in a row. Add G. Make 4.

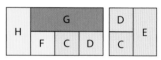

4. Sew H to the D/C/F/G unit. Add the C/D/E unit.

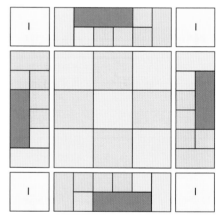

5. Arrange the units and the I squares. Then sew them together.

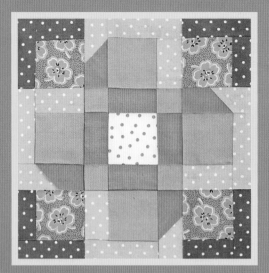

BLOCK 2

FABRIC REQUIREMENTS

Amounts listed are for 18 blocks because featured quilts (pages 26–31) are assembled with 35 blocks—18 of one block and 17 of another.

White polka dot: ¼ yard

Periwinkle: ⅝ yard

Dark pink: ½ yard

Pink polka dot: ¾ yard

Blue polka dot: ⅝ yard

Green floral: ½ yard

CUTTING

White polka dot

Cut 2 strips 2½" × fabric width, then cut into 18 squares 2½" × 2½" (A).

Periwinkle

Cut 5 strips 2½" × fabric width, then cut into 72 squares 2½" × 2½" (B).

Cut 3 strips 1½" × fabric width, then cut into 72 squares 1½" × 1½" (C).

Dark pink

Cut 10 strips 1½" × fabric width, then cut into 72 rectangles 1½" × 2½" (D) and 72 E shapes (E template on page 46).

Pink polka dot

Cut 16 strips 1½" × fabric width, then cut into 72 rectangles 1½" × 2½" (F), 72 rectangles 1½" × 3½" (G), and 72 H shapes (H template on page 46).

Blue polka dot

Cut 11 strips 1½" × fabric width, then cut into 72 rectangles 1½" × 2½" (I) and 72 rectangles 1½" × 3½" (J).

Green floral

Cut 5 strips 2½" × fabric width, then cut into 72 squares 2½" × 2½" (K).

BLOCK CONSTRUCTION

Instructions are for constructing one block.

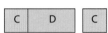

1. Sew 2 C's to the ends of a D. Make 2.

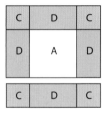

2. Sew 2 D's to an A.
Add the C/D/C units to D/A/D.

3. Sew E to H. Make 4.

4. Sew F to B. Add G. Make 4.

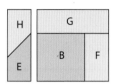

5. Sew E/H to B/F/G. Make 4.

6. Sew I to K. Add J. Make 4.

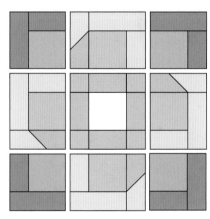

7. Arrange the units and sew them together.

BLOCK 3

FABRIC REQUIREMENTS

Amounts listed are for 18 blocks because featured quilts (pages 26–31) are assembled with 35 blocks—18 of one block and 17 of another.

Blue print: ½ yard

Green: 1 yard

Purple swirl print: ½ yard

Rust swirl print: ¾ yard

CUTTING

Blue print

Cut 2 strips 4¾″ × fabric width, then cut into 18 squares 4¾″ × 4¾″ (A).

Green

Cut 4 strips 3⅞″ × fabric width, then cut into 36 squares 3⅞″ × 3⅞″. Cut each square in half diagonally to yield 72 large triangles (B).

Cut 5 strips 2⅞″ × fabric width, then cut into 72 squares 2⅞″ × 2⅞″. Cut each square in half diagonally to yield 144 small triangles (C).

Purple swirl print

Cut 5 strips 2⅞″ × fabric width, then cut into 72 squares 2⅞″ × 2⅞″. Cut each square in half diagonally to yield 144 small triangles (D).

Rust swirl print

Cut 9 strips 2½″ × fabric width, then cut into 144 squares 2½″ × 2½″ (E).

BLOCK CONSTRUCTION

Instructions are for constructing one block.

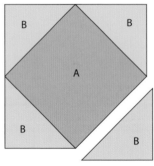

1. Sew 4 B's to A.

2. Sew C's to D's. Make 8. Sew 2 C/D's to E. Make 4.

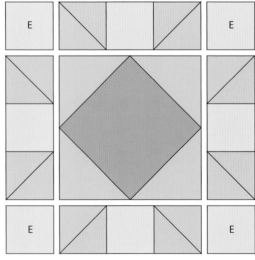

3. Arrange the units and the remaining E squares. Then sew them together.

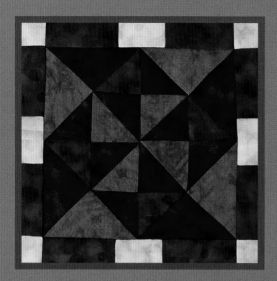

BLOCK 4

FABRIC REQUIREMENTS

Amounts listed are for 18 blocks because featured quilts (pages 26–31) are assembled with 35 blocks—18 of one block and 17 of another.

Avocado mottle print: 1 yard
Blue-violet jacquard: 1⅛ yards
Red-violet jacquard: ⅞ yard
Peach jacquard: ⅜ yard

CUTTING

Avocado mottle print

Cut 2 strips 4″ × fabric width, then cut into 18 squares 4″ × 4″. Cut each square in half twice diagonally to yield 72 small triangles (A).

Cut 3 strips 5¼″ × fabric width, then cut into 18 squares 5¼″ × 5¼″. Cut each square in half twice diagonally to yield 72 large triangles (D).

Blue-violet jacquard

Cut 4 strips 4″ × fabric width, then cut into 36 squares 4″ × 4″. Cut each square in half twice diagonally to yield 144 small triangles (B).

Cut 3 strips 5¼″ × fabric width, then cut into 18 squares 5¼″ × 5¼″. Cut each square in half twice diagonally to yield 72 large triangles (E).

Red-violet jacquard

Cut 12 strips 1½″ × fabric width, then cut into 144 rectangles 1½″ × 3½″ (F).

Cut 2 strips 4″ × fabric width, then cut into 18 squares 4″ × 4″. Cut each square in half twice diagonally to yield 72 small triangles (C).

Peach jacquard

Cut 7 strips 1½″ × fabric width, then cut into 72 squares 1½″ × 1½″ (H) and 72 rectangles 1½″ × 2½″ (G).

BLOCK CONSTRUCTION

Instructions are for constructing one block.

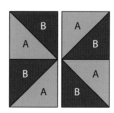

1. Sew 4 A's to 4 B's to make a pinwheel square.

2. Sew B to C. Make 4.

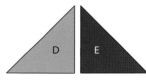

3. Sew D to E. Make 4.

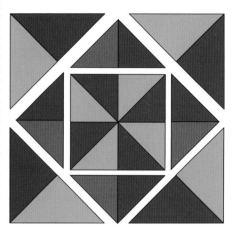

4. Arrange and sew the units together.

5. Sew 2 F's to G. Make 4.

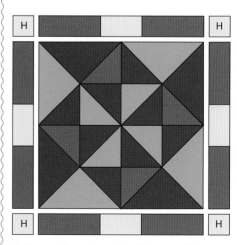

6. Arrange the units and the H squares. Then sew them together.

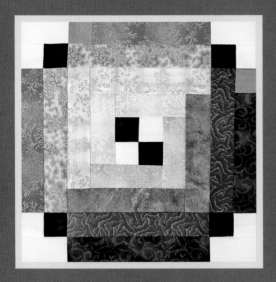

BLOCK 5

FABRIC REQUIREMENTS

Amounts listed are for 18 blocks because featured quilts (pages 26–31) are assembled with 35 blocks—18 of one block and 17 of another.

Black: ¼ yard

White: ½ yard

Gray: ¼ yard

Light green print: ¼ yard

Medium green mottle print: ⅓ yard

Teal variegated print: ⅓ yard

Dark green print: ⅜ yard

Ivory print: ¼ yard

Butter print: ⅓ yard

Tan print: ⅓ yard

Bronze print: ⅓ yard

CUTTING

Black

Cut 4 strips 1½" × fabric width, then cut into 108 squares 1½" × 1½" (A).

White

Cut 8 strips 1½" × fabric width, then cut into 108 squares 1½" × 1½" (B) and 72 rectangles 1½" × 2½" (C).

Gray

Cut 2 strips 1½" × fabric width, then cut into 36 squares 1½" × 1½" (D).

Light green print

Cut 3 strips 1½" × fabric width, then cut into 36 rectangles 1½" × 3½" (E).

Medium green mottle print

Cut 5 strips 1½" × fabric width, then cut into 36 rectangles 1½" × 5½" (G).

Teal variegated print

Cut 6 strips 1½" × fabric width, then cut into 36 rectangles 1½" × 6½" (I).

Dark green print

Cut 6 strips 1½" × fabric width, then cut into 18 rectangles 1½" × 5½" (K) and 18 rectangles 1½" × 6½" (L).

Ivory print

Cut 3 strips 1½" × fabric width, then cut into 36 rectangles 1½" × 3½" (F).

Butter print

Cut 5 strips 1½" × fabric width, then cut into 36 rectangles 1½" × 5½" (H).

Tan print

Cut 6 strips 1½" × fabric width, then cut into 36 rectangles 1½" × 6½" (J).

Bronze print

Cut 6 strips 1½" × fabric width, then cut into 18 rectangles 1½" × 5½" (M) and 18 rectangles 1½" × 6½" (N).

BLOCK CONSTRUCTION

Instructions are for constructing one block.

1. Sew 2 A's and 2 B's together to make a four-patch unit.

2. Sew an A to a B. Add a C to the top. Make 2.

3. Sew an A to a B. Add a C to the bottom. Make 2.

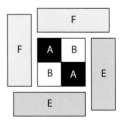

4. Sew 2 E's and 2 F's to the four-patch square. (Refer to the sidebar on page 17 for construction guidance.)

CONSTRUCTION

1. Stop the first seam ¼" from the square's edge.

2. Add the second rectangle.

3. Add the third rectangle.

4. Add the final rectangle and stop the seam ¼" from the square's edge.

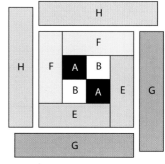

5. Align the short side of the fourth rectangle with the long side of the first and sew them together.

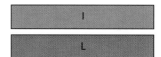

5. Add 2 G's and 2 H's.

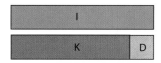

6. Sew an I to an L.

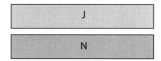

7. Sew a J to an N.

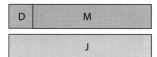

8. Sew a D to a K. Add an I.

9. Sew a D to an M. Add a J.

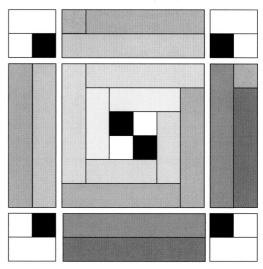

10. Arrange the units and sew them together.

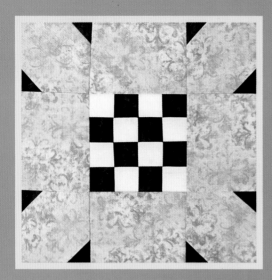

BLOCK 6

FABRIC REQUIREMENTS

Amounts listed are for 18 blocks because featured quilts (pages 26–31) are assembled with 35 blocks—18 of one block and 17 of another.

White: ⅓ yard

Black: ½ yard

Turquoise print: 1½ yards

CUTTING

White

Cut 5 strips 1½" × fabric width, then cut into 144 squares 1½" × 1½" (B).

Black

Cut 5 strips 1½" × fabric width, then cut into 144 squares 1½" × 1½" (A).

Cut 5 strips 1½" × fabric width, then cut into 144 squares 1½" × 1½" (C).

Turquoise print

Cut 8 strips 3½" × fabric width, then cut into 72 rectangles 3½" × 4½" (E).

Cut 6 strips 3½" × fabric width, then cut into 72 squares 3½" × 3½" (D).

BLOCK CONSTRUCTION

Instructions are for constructing one block.

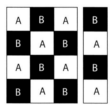

1. Sew 8 A's to 8 B's to make a checkerboard unit.

2. Sew 2 C's to a D. Make 4. (Refer to the sidebar for construction guidance.)

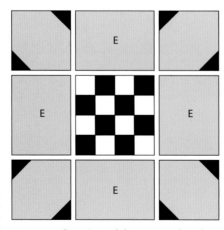

3. Arrange the units and the E rectangles. Then sew them together.

CONSTRUCTION

1. Draw a diagonal line from corner to corner on the wrong side of all the C squares. Place a C square on a corner of a D square, right sides together. Sew on the drawn diagonal line.

2. Trim the excess fabric, leaving a ¼" seam allowance.

3. Add a C square to the opposite corner of the D square.

BLOCK 7

FABRIC REQUIREMENTS

Amounts listed are for 18 blocks because featured quilts (pages 26–31) are assembled with 35 blocks—18 of one block and 17 of another.

Blue mottle print: ¼ yard

Green print: ⅝ yard

Gold print: ½ yard

Ivory print: 1 yard

Light blue mottle print: 1 yard

Hot pink print: ⅓ yard

CUTTING

Blue mottle print

Cut 2 strips 2½" × fabric width, then cut into 18 squares 2½" × 2½" (A).

Green print

Cut 5 strips 2½" × fabric width, then cut into 72 squares 2½" × 2½" (B).

Cut 3 strips 1½" × fabric width, then cut into 72 squares 1½" × 1½" (C).

Gold print

Cut 5 strips 1½" × fabric width, then cut into 144 squares 1½" × 1½" (D).

Cut 2 strips 3¼" × fabric width, then cut into 18 squares 3¼" × 3¼". Cut each square in half twice diagonally to yield 72 triangles (G).

Ivory print

Cut 3 strips 1½" × fabric width, then cut into 72 squares 1½" × 1½" (E).

Cut 2 strips 3¼" × fabric width, then cut into 18 squares 3¼" × 3¼". Cut each square in half twice diagonally to yield 72 triangles (I).

Cut 5 strips 2½" × fabric width, then cut into 72 squares 2½" × 2½" (J).

Light blue mottle print

Cut 2 strips 3¼" × fabric width, then cut into 18 squares 3¼" × 3¼". Cut each

square in half twice diagonally to yield 72 triangles (H).

Cut 8 strips 2½" × fabric width, then cut into 72 rectangles 2½" × 4½" (K).

Hot pink print

Cut 2 strips 3¼" × fabric width, then cut into 18 squares 3¼" × 3¼". Cut each square in half twice diagonally to yield 72 triangles (F).

BLOCK CONSTRUCTION

Instructions are for constructing one block.

1. Sew a C to a D and a D to an E. Sew the C/D unit to the D/E unit to make a four-patch unit. Make 4.

2. Sew a C/D/D/E unit to each side of a B. Make 2. Sew a B to each side of A. Arrange the units and sew them together.

3. Sew an H to an F and an H to a G. Sew them together. Make 2.

4. Sew a K to the top and bottom of an H/F/H/G unit. Make 2.

5. Sew an I to an F and an I to a G. Make 2.

6. Sew a J to each side of an I/F/I/G unit. Make 2.

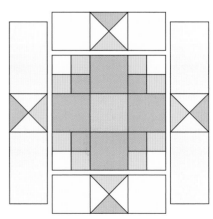

7. Arrange the units and sew them together.

BLOCK 8

FABRIC REQUIREMENTS

Amounts listed are for 18 blocks because featured quilts (pages 26–31) are assembled with 35 blocks—18 of one block and 17 of another.

Gold print: ¾ yard

Yellow mottle print: ½ yard

Hot pink print: 1⅛ yards

Blue print: ½ yard

CUTTING

Gold print

Cut 2 strips 2½″ × fabric width, then cut into 18 squares 2½″ × 2½″ (A).

Cut 3 strips 2⅞″ × fabric width, then cut into 36 squares 2⅞″ × 2⅞″. Cut each square in half diagonally to yield 72 triangles (C).

Cut 5 strips 1½″ × fabric width, then cut into 144 squares 1½″ × 1½″ (F).

Yellow mottle print

Cut 5 strips 2½″ × fabric width, then cut into 72 squares 2½″ × 2½″ (B).

Hot pink print

Cut 5 strips 1½″ × fabric width, then cut into 144 squares 1½″ × 1½″ (E).

Cut 8 strips 2½″ × fabric width, then cut into 72 rectangles 2½″ × 4½″ (G).

Cut 3 strips 2⅞″ × fabric width, then cut into 36 squares 2⅞″ × 2⅞″. Cut each square in half diagonally to yield 72 triangles (D).

Blue print

Cut 5 strips 2½″ × fabric width, then cut into 72 squares 2½″ × 2½″ (H).

BLOCK CONSTRUCTION

Instructions are for constructing one block.

1. Sew a C to a D to make a square. Make 4.

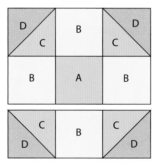

2. Sew a C/D unit to each side of a B. Make 2. Sew a B to each side of A. Arrange the units and sew them together.

3. Sew an E to an F. Make 2. Sew E/F units to each side of a G. Make 4.

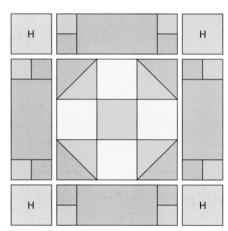

4. Arrange the units and the H squares. Then sew them together.

BLOCK 9

FABRIC REQUIREMENTS

Amounts listed are for 18 blocks because featured quilts (pages 26–31) are assembled with 35 blocks—18 of one block and 17 of another.

Green batik: 1½ yards

Brown batik: ½ yard

Peach batik: ⅝ yard

CUTTING

Green batik

Cut 7 strips 4″ × fabric width, then cut into 72 squares 4″ × 4″ (A).

Cut 6 strips 3½″ × fabric width, then cut into 72 squares 3½″ × 3½″. Cut each square into a C shape (C template on page 46).

Brown batik

Cut 5 strips 2⅞″ × fabric width, then cut into 72 squares 2⅞″ × 2⅞″. Cut each square in half diagonally to yield 144 triangles (E).

Peach batik

Cut 4 strips 2″ × fabric width, then cut into 72 squares 2″ × 2″ (B).

Cut 3 strips 2⅞″ × fabric width, then cut into 36 squares 2⅞″ × 2⅞″. Cut each square in half diagonally to yield 72 triangles (D).

BLOCK CONSTRUCTION

Instructions are for constructing one block.

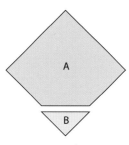

1. Sew a B to an A to make a square. Make 4. (Refer to the Construction sidebar on page 18 for construction guidance.)

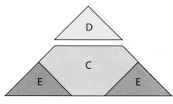

2. Sew 2 E's to a C. Add a D. Make 4.

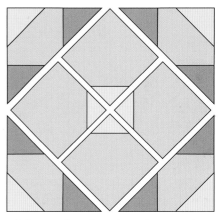

3. Arrange the units and sew them together.

BLOCK 10

FABRIC REQUIREMENTS

Amounts listed are for 18 blocks because featured quilts (pages 26–31) are assembled with 35 blocks—18 of one block and 17 of another.

Gold batik: ⅝ yard

Lavender batik: ½ yard

Purple batik: ½ yard

Peach batik: 1 yard

Green batik: ⅝ yard

CUTTING

Gold batik

Cut 2 strips 4½″ × fabric width, then cut into 18 squares 4½″ × 4½″ (A).

Cut 5 strips 1½″ × fabric width, then cut into 144 squares 1½″ × 1½″ (D).

Lavender batik

Cut 8 strips 1½″ × fabric width, then cut into 72 rectangles 1½″ × 4½″ (B).

Purple batik

Cut 8 strips 1½″ × fabric width, then cut into 216 squares 1½″ × 1½″ (C).

Peach batik

Cut 12 strips 2½″ × fabric width, then cut into 144 rectangles 2½″ × 3⅝″. Cut 72 rectangles into shape E and 72 rectangles into shape E reverse (E template on page 46). (Refer to the Cutting Tip for guidance.)

CUTTING TIP

Trace template E on the right side of the fabric for shape E. Trace template E on the wrong side of the fabric for shape E reverse.

Green batik

Cut 3 strips 5¼″ × fabric width, then cut into 18 squares 5¼″ × 5¼″. Cut each square in half twice diagonally to yield 72 triangles (G).

BLOCK CONSTRUCTION

Instructions are for constructing one block.

1. Sew a C to each end of a B. Make 2.

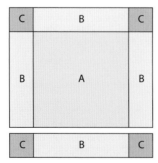

2. Sew a B to each side of A. Sew a C/B/C unit to each side of B/A/B.

3. Sew a C to a D. Make 2. Sew together to make a four-patch unit. Make 4.

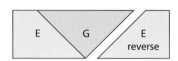

4. Sew an E to a G and add an E reverse. Make 4.

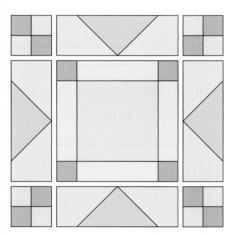

5. Arrange the units and sew them together.

BLOCK 11

FABRIC REQUIREMENTS

Amounts listed are for 18 blocks because featured quilts (pages 26–31) are assembled with 35 blocks—18 of one block and 17 of another.

Pink: 1½ yards

Burgundy print: ⅜ yard

Olive print: ½ yard

Dark green print: ½ yard

CUTTING

Pink

Cut 3 strips 3½″ × fabric width, then cut into 36 squares 3½″ × 3½″ (A).

Cut 5 strips 1½″ × fabric width, then cut into 144 squares 1½″ × 1½″ (B).

Cut 5 strips 1½″ × fabric width, then cut into 144 squares 1½″ × 1½″ (C).

Cut 8 strips 2½″ × fabric width, then cut into 72 rectangles 2½″ × 4½″ (D).

Burgundy print

Cut 3 strips 3½″ × fabric width, then cut into 36 squares 3½″ × 3½″ (F).

Olive print

Cut 5 strips 1½″ × fabric width, then cut into 144 squares 1½″ × 1½″ (E). Cut 18 leaves (leaf template on page 46).

Dark green print

Cut 5 strips 2½″ × fabric width, then cut into 72 squares 2½″ × 2½″ (G).

BLOCK CONSTRUCTION

Instructions are for constructing one block.

1. Sew 4 C's to an F to make a square. Make 2. (Refer to the Construction sidebar on page 18 for construction guidance.)

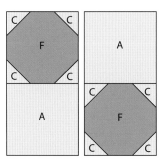

2. Sew a C/F square to an A. Make 2. Sew the units together.

3. Sew a B to an E. Make 2. Sew a B/E unit to each end of a D. Make 4.

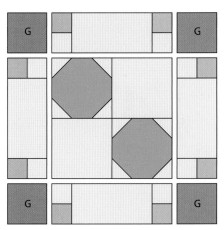

4. Arrange the units and the G squares. Then sew them together.

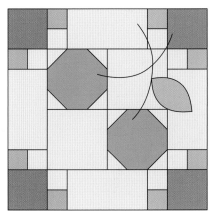

5. With the air-soluble pen, mark the stems. Stitch along the marked lines with dark green thread. (Refer to the general instructions for Machine Embroidery on page 7.)

6. Pin the leaf in place. Stitch in place. (Refer to the general instructions for Hand Appliqué on page 7.)

BLOCK 12

FABRIC REQUIREMENTS

Amounts listed are for 18 blocks because featured quilts (pages 26–31) are assembled with 35 blocks—18 of one block and 17 of another.

Yellow print: 1 yard

Dark green print: 1⅔ yards

CUTTING

Yellow print

Cut 5 strips 2½″ × fabric width, then cut into 72 squares 2½″ × 2½″ (B).

Cut 10 strips 1½″ × fabric width, then cut into 288 squares 1½″ × 1½″ (C).

Dark green print

Cut 2 strips 2½″ × fabric width, then cut into 18 squares 2½″ × 2½″ (A).

Cut 16 strips 1½″ × fabric width, then cut into 72 squares 1½″ × 1½″ (E) and 216 rectangles 1½″ × 2½″ (D).

Cut 6 strips 3½″ × fabric width, then cut into 72 squares 3½″ × 3½″ (F).

BLOCK CONSTRUCTION

Instructions are for constructing one block.

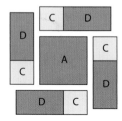

1. Sew a C to a D. Make 4.
Sew the C/D units to A.
(Refer to the sidebar for construction guidance.)

CONSTRUCTION

1. Stop the first seam ¼″ from the square's edge. Backstitch.

2. Add the second rectangle unit.

3. Add the third rectangle unit.

4. Add the final rectangle unit and stop the seam ¼″ from the square's edge. Backstitch.

5. Align the short side of the fourth rectangle with the long side of the first and sew together. Backstick at the start.

2. Sew a C to an E and add a B. Make 4.

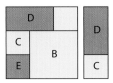

3. Sew a C to a D. Make 8. Sew 2 C/D units to a
C/E/B unit. Make 4.

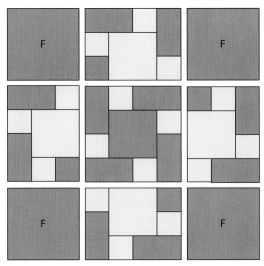

4. Arrange the units and the F squares.
Then sew them together.

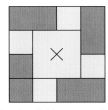

5. With the air-soluble pen, mark the flower
centers. Stitch along the marked lines with dark
green thread. (Refer to the general instructions for
Machine Embroidery on page 7.)

QUILT 1

55½″ × 75½″

BLOCK REQUIREMENTS

18 #1 Blocks (page 12)

17 #2 Blocks (page 13)

MATERIALS NEEDED

Light yellow: ⅓ yard

Medium yellow: ½ yard

Binding: 1¼ yards or 270″ premade bias binding

Batting: 63″ × 83″

Backing: 3⅜ yards

CONSTRUCTION

1. Starting with Block 1 in the upper left corner, sew the completed blocks together, alternating between Block 1 and Block 2. You will end up with 5 across and 7 down.

2. Piece the yellow fabrics together as desired to make 2 strips 3″ × 50½″. Sew the strips to the top and bottom of the quilt top.

3. Piece the yellow fabrics together as desired to make 2 strips 3″ × 75½″. Sew the strips to the sides of the quilt top.

4. Refer to General Instructions (pages 7–9) as you mark, layer, pin, and quilt the quilt. Bind the quilt with 2⅛″-wide bias strips pieced together to total approximately 270″.

QUILT 2

55½" × 75½"

BLOCK REQUIREMENTS

18 #3 Blocks (page 14)

17 #4 Blocks (page 15)

MATERIALS NEEDED

Navy jacquard: ¾ yard

Binding: 1¼ yards or 270"
premade bias binding

Batting: 63" × 83"

Backing: 3⅜ yards

CONSTRUCTION

1. Starting with Block 3 in the
   upper left corner, sew the
   completed blocks together,
   alternating between Block 3 and
   Block 4. You will end up with 5
   across and 7 down.

2. Piece the navy jacquard fabric
   together as desired to make 2
   strips 3" × 50½". Sew the strips
   to the top and bottom of the
   quilt top.

3. Piece the navy jacquard fabric
   together as desired to make 2
   strips 3" × 75½". Sew the strips
   to the sides of the quilt top.

4. Refer to General Instructions
   (pages 7–9) as you mark, layer,
   pin, and quilt the quilt. Bind the
   quilt with 2⅛"-wide bias strips
   pieced together to total approximately 270".

QUILT 3

55½″ × 75½″

BLOCK REQUIREMENTS

17 #5 Blocks (page 16)

18 #6 Blocks (page 18)

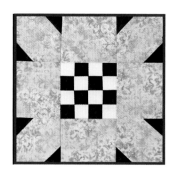

MATERIALS NEEDED

Green print: ¾ yard

Binding: 1¼ yards or 270″ premade bias binding

Batting: 63″ × 83″

Backing: 3⅜ yards

CONSTRUCTION

1. Starting with Block 6 in the upper left corner, sew the completed blocks together, alternating between Block 5 and Block 6. You will end up with 5 across and 7 down.

2. Piece the green print fabric together as desired to make 2 strips 3″ × 50½″. Sew the strips to the top and bottom of the quilt top.

3. Piece the green print fabric together as desired to make 2 strips 3″ × 75½″. Sew the strips to the sides of the quilt top.

4. Refer to General Instructions (pages 7–9) as you mark, layer, pin, and quilt the quilt. Bind the quilt with 2⅛″-wide bias strips pieced together to total approximately 270″.

QUILT 4

55½" × 75½"

BLOCK REQUIREMENTS

17 #7 Blocks (page 19)

18 #8 Blocks (page 20)

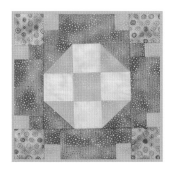

MATERIALS NEEDED

Hot pink print: ¾ yard

Binding: 1¼ yards or 270" premade bias binding

Batting: 63" × 83"

Backing: 3⅜ yards

CONSTRUCTION

1. Starting with Block 8 in the upper left corner, sew the completed blocks together, alternating between Block 7 and Block 8. You will end up with 5 across and 7 down.

2. Piece the hot pink print fabric together as desired to make 2 strips 3" × 50½". Sew the strips to the top and bottom of the quilt top.

3. Piece the hot pink print fabric together as desired to make 2 strips 3" × 75½". Sew the strips to the sides of the quilt top.

4. Refer to General Instructions (pages 7–9) as you mark, layer, pin, and quilt the quilt. Bind the quilt with 2⅛"-wide bias strips pieced together to total approximately 270".

QUILT 5

55½" × 75½"

BLOCK REQUIREMENTS

18 #9 Blocks (page 21)

17 #10 Blocks (page 22)

MATERIALS NEEDED

Green batik: ¾ yard

Binding: 1¼ yards or 270" premade bias binding

Batting: 63" × 83"

Backing: 3⅜ yards

CONSTRUCTION

1. Starting with Block 9 in the upper left corner, sew the completed blocks together, alternating between Block 9 and Block 10. You will end up with 5 across and 7 down.

2. Piece the green batik fabric together as desired to make 2 strips 3" × 50½". Sew the strips to the top and bottom of the quilt top.

3. Piece the green batik fabric together as desired to make 2 strips 3" × 75½". Sew the strips to the sides of the quilt top.

4. Refer to General Instructions (pages 7–9) as you mark, layer, pin, and quilt the quilt. Bind the quilt with 2⅛"-wide bias strips pieced together to total approximately 270".

QUILT 6

55½" × 75½"

BLOCK REQUIREMENTS

17 #11 Blocks (page 23)

18 #12 Blocks (page 24)

MATERIALS NEEDED

Pink print: ¾ yard

Binding: 1 yard

Batting: 63" × 83"

Backing: 3⅜ yards

CONSTRUCTION

1. Starting with Block 12 in the upper left corner, sew the completed blocks together, alternating between Block 11 and Block 12. You will end up with 5 across and 7 down.

2. Piece the pink print fabric together as desired to make 2 strips 3" × 50½". Sew the strips to the top and bottom of the quilt top.

3. Piece the pink print fabric together as desired to make 2 strips 3" × 75½". Sew the strips to the sides of the quilt top.

4. Refer to General Instructions (pages 7–9) as you mark, layer, pin, and quilt the quilt. Bind the quilt with 2⅛"-wide bias strips pieced together to total approximately 270".

Alternate Combinations

BLOCKS #1 AND #11 PALETTES

Block #1	Block #11
yellow	yellow
yellow print	pink
green	green
pink	blue
blue	red

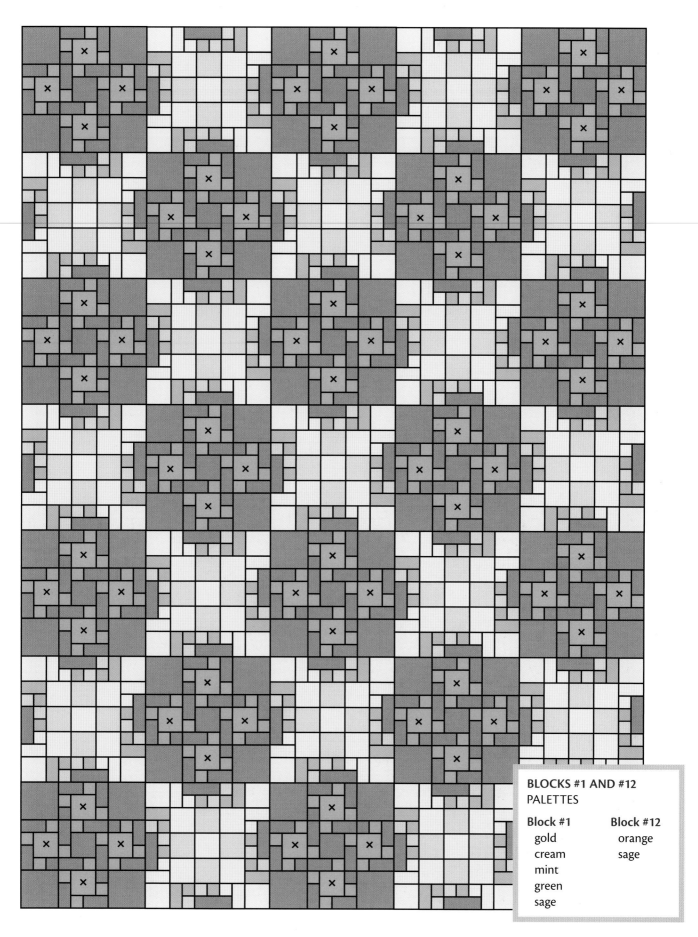

BLOCKS #1 AND #12
PALETTES

Block #1	Block #12
gold	orange
cream	sage
mint	
green	
sage	

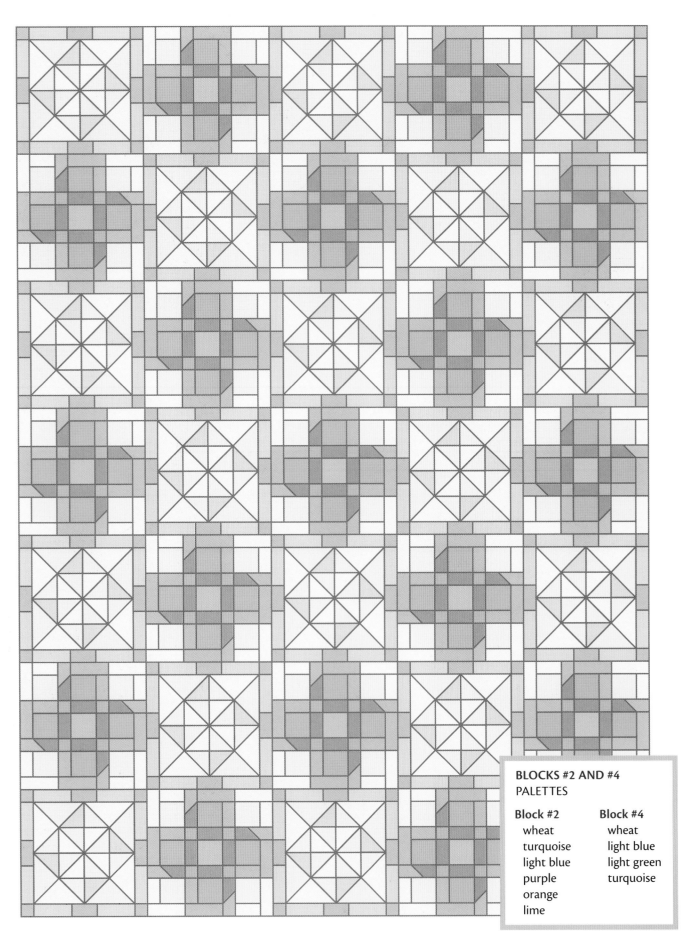

BLOCKS #2 AND #4
PALETTES

Block #2	Block #4
wheat	wheat
turquoise	light blue
light blue	light green
purple	turquoise
orange	
lime	

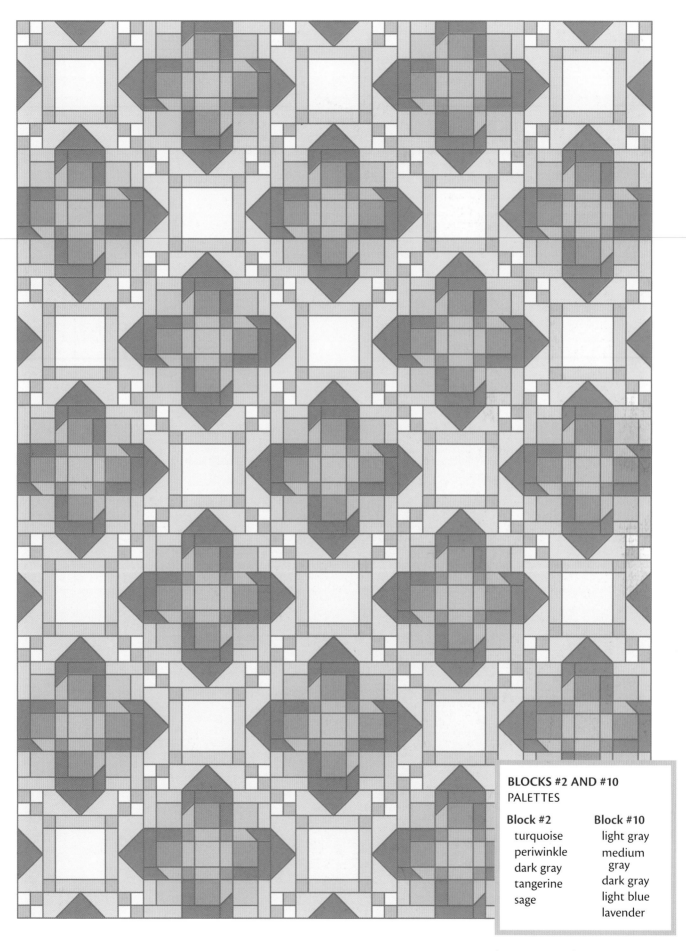

BLOCKS #2 AND #10 PALETTES

Block #2	Block #10
turquoise	light gray
periwinkle	medium gray
dark gray	dark gray
tangerine	light blue
sage	lavender

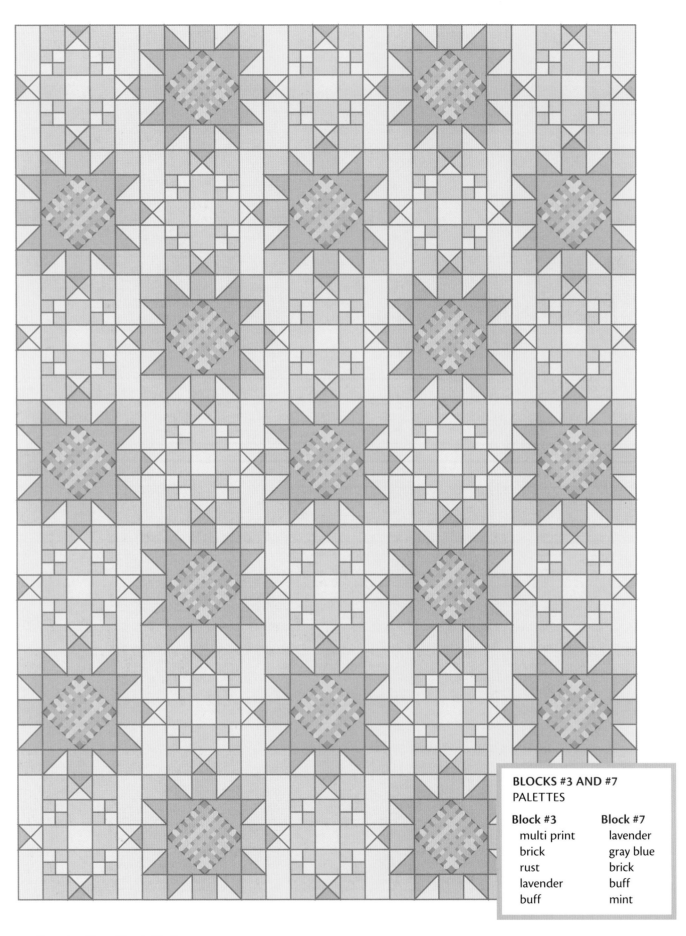

BLOCKS #3 AND #7
PALETTES

Block #3	Block #7
multi print	lavender
brick	gray blue
rust	brick
lavender	buff
buff	mint

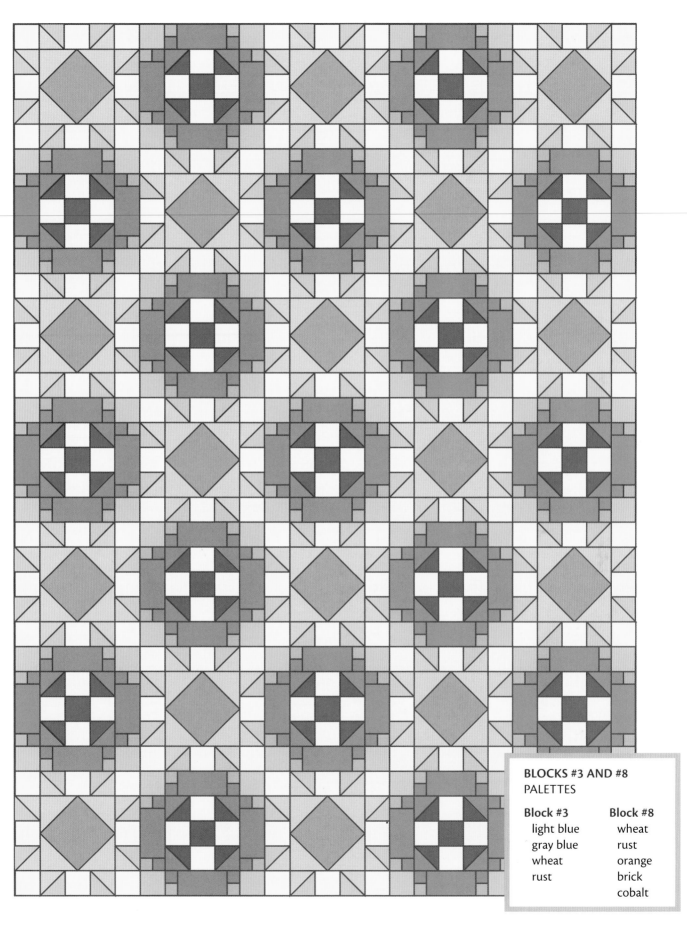

BLOCKS #3 AND #8
PALETTES

Block #3	Block #8
light blue	wheat
gray blue	rust
wheat	orange
rust	brick
	cobalt

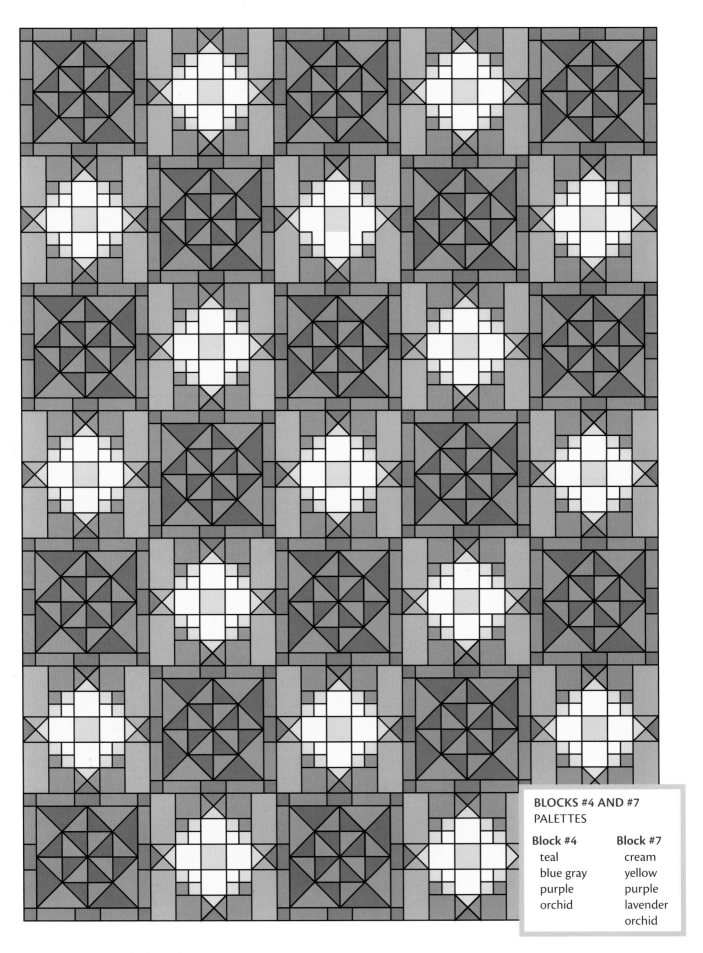

BLOCKS #4 AND #7 PALETTES

Block #4	Block #7
teal	cream
blue gray	yellow
purple	purple
orchid	lavender
	orchid

BLOCKS #4 AND #8
PALETTES

Block #4	Block #8
lavender	orchid
light gray	cream
medium gray	gold
orchid	medium gray

BLOCKS #5 AND #10
PALETTES

Block #5	Block #10
wheat	white
sage	white pin
lavender	dot
peach	green
light blue	periwinkle
green	wheat
white	

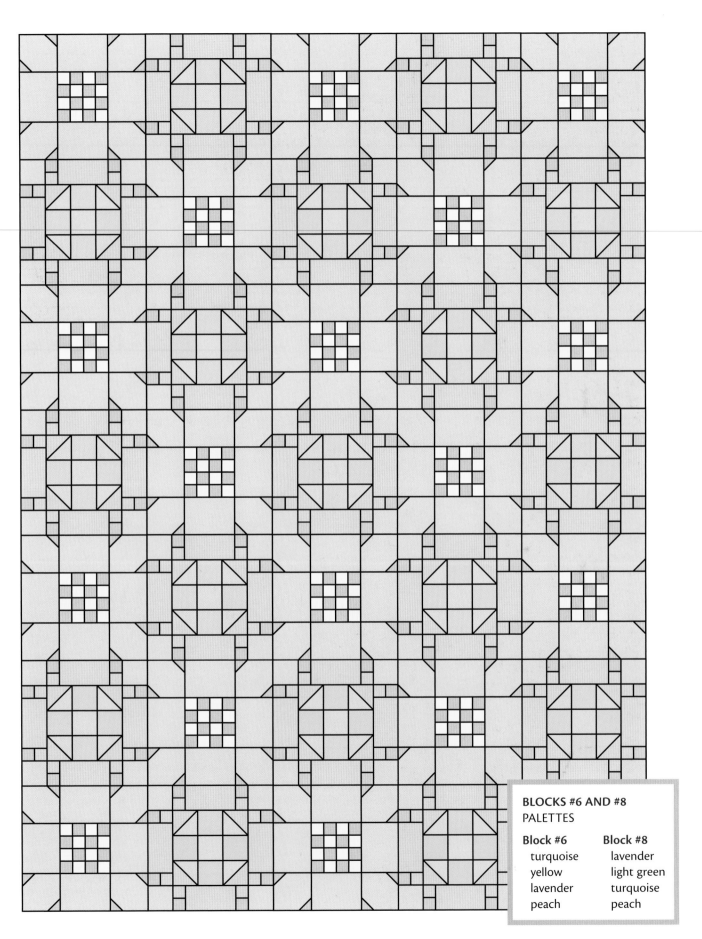

BLOCKS #6 AND #8
PALETTES

Block #6	Block #8
turquoise	lavender
yellow	light green
lavender	turquoise
peach	peach

BLOCKS #6 AND #9
PALETTES

Block #6	Block #9
light blue	cobalt
medium blue	fuchsia
fuchsia	tan
variegated	black

BLOCKS #6 AND #12
PALETTES

Block #6	Block #12
white	apricot
turquoise	pink
light green	
apricot	

BLOCKS #8 AND #10
PALETTES

Block #8	Block #10
gold	multi print
yellow	lavender
polka dot	rose
turquoise	turquoise
wheat	wheat

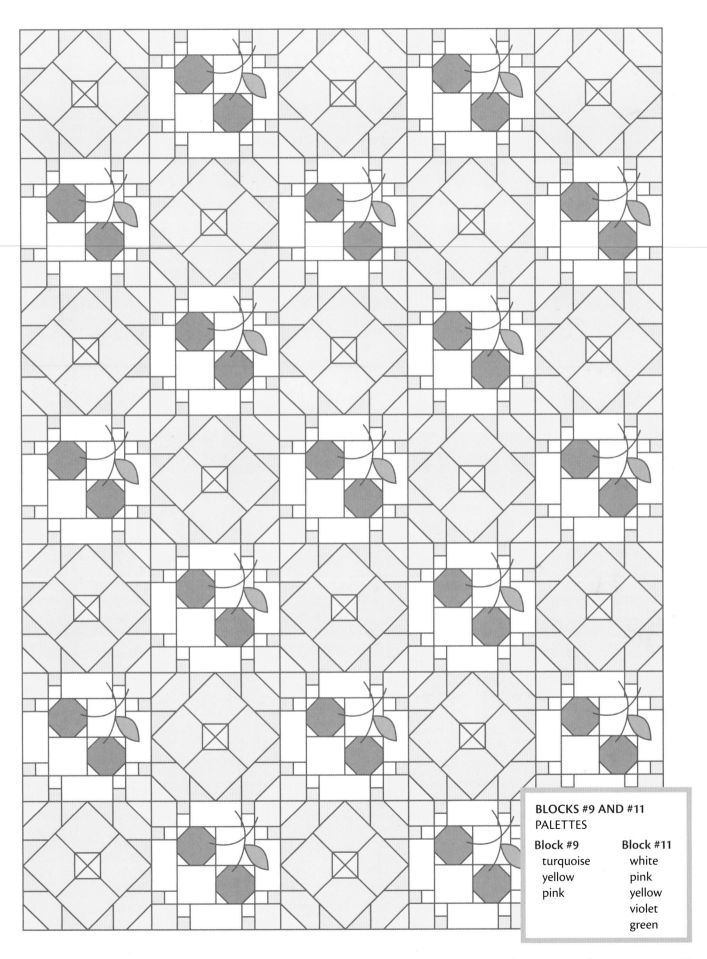

**BLOCKS #9 AND #11
PALETTES**

Block #9	Block #11
turquoise	white
yellow	pink
pink	yellow
	violet
	green

Templates

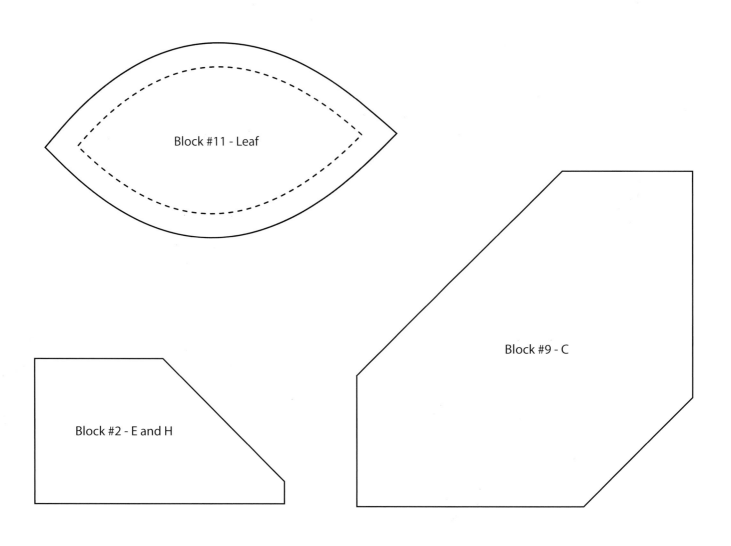

Block #11 - Leaf

Block #9 - C

Block #2 - E and H

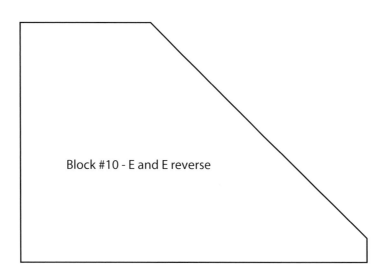

Block #10 - E and E reverse

About the Author

Trice Boerens is a designer who lives and works in the foot-hills of the Wasatch Mountains in Ogden, Utah. She has authored books on quilting, needlework, and papercrafting. When not working, she enjoys cycling and reading biographies of famous Americans (not at the same time).

She can trace her inspiration for quilting to a college professor who was fascinated by Arabic tile patterns. As his student, she reviewed hundreds of photos of walls, floors, ceilings, and roofs that had tile patterns based on square, radial, and triangular grids. After that semester, "something-something" years ago, she wanted to spend all of her free time making fabric puzzles.

Great Titles *from* C&T PUBLISHING

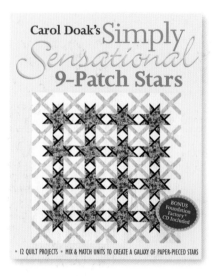

Available at your local retailer or **www.ctpub.com** *or* **800.284.1114**

For a list of other fine books from C&T Publishing, ask for a free catalog:

C&T PUBLISHING, INC.
P.O. Box 1456
Lafayette, CA 94549
(800) 284-1114

Email: ctinfo@ctpub.com
Website: www.ctpub.com

C&T Publishing's professional photography services are now available to the public. Visit us at www.ctmediaservices.com.

Tips and Techniques can be found at www.ctpub.com > Consumer Resources > Quiltmaking Basics: Tips & Techniques for Quiltmaking & More

For quilting supplies:

COTTON PATCH
1025 Brown Ave.
Lafayette, CA 94549
Store: (925) 284-1177
Mail order: (925) 283-7883

Email: CottonPa@aol.com
Website: www.quiltusa.com

Note: Fabrics used in the quilts shown may not be currently available, as fabric manufacturers keep most fabrics in print for only a short time.